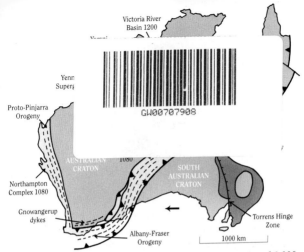

Above: *The assembly of Australian cratons between 1,300 and 1,000 million years ago.*

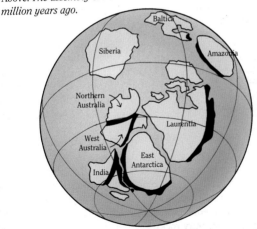

The supercontinent Rodinia, about 750 million years ago, showing the main areas of mountain building (in black).

Antarctica. The collision of the West Australian and Mawson Cratons took place as part of the assembly of a supercontinent called Rodinia.

Another continent probably collided with the West Australian Craton about 1100 million years ago, and a similar mountain range, called the Pinjarra Orogen, began to form along the western edge of the Yilgarn Craton. Most of the rocks that formed then now lie buried deep beneath today's coastal plains. The Darling Fault, which can be traced from near Shark Bay down to the south coast, marked the edge of this mountain range. During the following 500 million years, magma was periodically squeezed into surrounding rocks, which between Cape Naturaliste and Cape Leeuwin were then slowly metamorphosed into gneiss. About 750 million years ago Rodinia began to break up into smaller plates. These reassembled into a new supercontinent called Gondwana about 250 million years later. It included Australia, Antarctica, Greater India, New Zealand, South America, Africa and parts of South-East Asia.

About 430 million years ago, the Darling Fault became very active again and formed an elongate trough called the Perth Basin. Over the next 300 million years, the basin filled up with more than 10 kilometres of sedimentary rocks. During part of this time, around 295 million years ago, Australia was close to the South Pole and extensive icecaps covered the South-West. Glaciers carved valleys in the landscape and blankets of broken and ground-up rocks were deposited as the ice melted. A rift developed within Gondwana's crust around 135 million years ago, slowly tearing from north to south, and Greater India drifted away from Australia as a result. Magma was generated as the crust split, reaching the Earth's surface and forming extensive flows of basalt lava in the South-West. Rifting then commenced along the present day south

4

GEOLOGY &
LANDFORMS
of the South-West

by Iain Copp

DEPARTMENT OF
Conservation
AND LAND MANAGEMENT

Conserving the nature of WA

More than 3700 million years of geological history is recorded in rocks of the South-West.

The oldest rocks are found in the Yilgarn Craton, a large piece of the Earth's crust that underlies most of the South-West. It formed between about 3700 and 2400 million years ago by the joining together of several smaller pieces of crust, resulting in a vast, geologically stable new continent. Huge volumes of molten rock (magma) were produced during this time, either finding their way to the surface to be erupted from volcanoes, or crystallising many kilometres below the surface. Other parts of the craton were subject to extreme pressures and temperatures and were transformed, or metamorphosed, to other types of rocks, such as gneiss. Under the most extreme conditions, some rocks began to melt and form migmatites. All these types of rocks can be found throughout the Darling Range and the Wheatbelt.

Between about 2000 and 1800 million years ago, the Yilgarn Craton collided with the Pilbara Craton to the north, forming a large new continent known as the West Australian Craton. This slowly drifted north-eastward until, 450 million years later, it collided with another large continent, the Mawson Craton (comprising the South Australian Craton and East Antarctica), which was drifting westward. This collision took place about 1345 million years ago along most of what is now the south coast. The Mawson Craton was thrust over the West Australian Craton, producing a huge thickness of crumpled crust, similar to the way that the Himalayas formed when India collided with Asia. Igneous rocks such as granite were formed during this upheaval and older granites were metamorphosed into gneiss. Slices of crust containing sedimentary rocks, such as The Barrens, were buried within this collision zone. The roots of this mountain range are known as the Albany-Fraser Orogen, and can be traced into

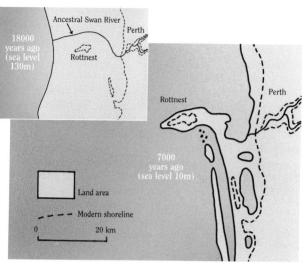

The South-West coast was subject to periodic changes in sea level

coast about 15 million years later, as Antarctica separated from Australia. This splitting of the Earth's crust caused the southern part of the South-West to be gently uplifted several times over about the next 35 million years.

Following the separation, the newly formed coastline of the South-West was then subject to periodic changes in sea level, the hinterland being sometimes covered by warm shallow seas. During the Eocene, about 40 million years ago, such a sea covered much of the South-West and was rich in sponges and other marine organisms. In the last two million years, during the Pleistocene, the polar icecaps have contracted and expanded many times, making the sea level rise and fall repeatedly. Belts of coastal sand dunes have followed this forever-changing coastline, and have been preserved as limestone in the cliffs around the South-West's coastline.

EVOLUTION OF THE SOUTH-WESTERN LANDSCAPE

The landscape of the South-West is very old, having probably begun to develop about 295 million years ago when a large icecap covered most of its surface. During this time, Australia was close to the South Pole and glaciers carved broad deep valleys into the landscape. Over the next 200 million years, the Darling Fault was very active and parts of the Yilgarn Craton were uplifted, forming a hinterland to the Perth Basin, which was mostly under water. The effects of heat, cold and rain on this ancient land surface weathered and eroded the hills and valleys that were formed by glacial action. Slowly, the gently undulating hills that characterise the Darling Plateau began to form. Around 95 million years ago, an extensive system of rivers was established over much of the South-West, further eroding the underlying rocks and forming the drainage pattern that we see today.

The South-West experienced a moist, temperate to tropical climate about 65 million years ago, resulting in deep inland penetration of rain-bearing westerly winds. This lasted for about 30 million years (to the end of the Eocene era), with the rain and surface run-off continuing to erode the rocks. It was during this period that a huge rise in sea level occurred, flooding large areas of the hinterland along the south coast with a warm sea rich in sponges. Only the highest points, such as the Stirling Range, Porongurup Range and the Barren Ranges, remained above sea level, forming islands and peninsulas. Over several million years, the continuous buffeting action by waves gradually reduced their size and cut platforms into their slopes. Between about 40 and 25 million years ago, a tropical climate allowed deep weathering of the rocks to take place. Alternating wet and dry periods leached out the more soluble minerals, leaving behind deeply weathered rocks overlain by mottled soils and an iron-rich capping called duricrust (see pages 30-31).

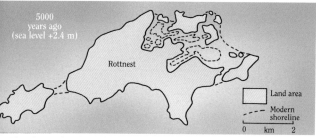

The shape of Rottnest has constantly changed due to rises and falls in the sea level

When the climate finally changed and started to dry out, most of the major river systems stopped flowing regularly. During the last two million years, the coastline changed position many times in response to the expansion and contraction of the polar icecaps. Sand dunes developed parallel to this changing coastline and are now represented by undulating limestone hills around coastal areas. Some of this limestone was partly dissolved by percolating rainwater and groundwater, forming caves and pinnacles. The sea level began to rise again about 18 000 years ago, as the last ice age ended. The islands and reefs offshore from Perth, which previously were connected to the mainland, then became separated. Old river valleys were slowly flooded and formed inlets along the coast, some finally being cut off from the ocean by the migration of recent sand dunes.

	Geological Interval	Years
SWAN COASTAL PLAIN		
Yalgorup Lake system	Quaternary	younger than 130 000
drowning of the coastline (e.g. Stokes Inlet)	Quaternary	younger than 130 000
Leeuwin-Naturaliste caves	Quaternary	younger than 1 million
Pinnacles	Quaternary	younger than 1 million
coastal limestone deposits	Quaternary	younger than 1 million
mineral sands	Pleistocene	300 000-100 000
aluminium and gold deposits in laterite	Eocene-Oligocene	40-25 million
laterite formation	Eocene-Oligocene	40-25 million
PERTH AND COLLIE BASINS		
Australia split from Greater India	Cretaceous	135 million
Bunbury Basalt	Cretaceous	135 million
Collie coal	Permian	280 million
glaciation	Permian	295 million

	Geological Interval	Years
LEEUWIN COMPLEX		
Gneiss and granites	Proterozoic	1100-530 million
ALBANY-FRASER OROGEN		
sponge-rich ocean sediments	Eocene	40 million
Australia split from Antarctica	Cretaceous	120 million
Stirling Range	Proterozoic	590 million
Porongurup Range	Proterozoic	1200 million
continental collision along the south coast	Proterozoic	1345-1140 million
The Barren Ranges	Proterozoic	1830 million
YILGARN CRATON		
Peak Charles	Proterozoic	2350 million
Greenbushes tantalum, lithium and tin	Archaean	2530 million
Darling Fault formed	Archaean	2600 million
Monadnocks (Darling Range Batholith)	Archaean	2650 million
Boddington volcanic rocks	Archaean	2700 million
Yilgarn Craton formed	Archaean	3700-2400 million

Rocks are classified into three types, according to their origin.

IGNEOUS ROCKS have solidified from molten rock (magma) formed deep within the Earth, which then moves upwards along cracks and faults. It may break through the Earth's surface and pour out as lava, forming volcanic rocks such as basalt or rhyolite. Pyroclastic deposits ('tuffs') are the accumulations of ash and other material (including pumice) produced by explosive volcanic eruptions. Magma that does not reach the Earth's surface is injected ('intruded') into pre-existing rocks. Just below the Earth's surface this may take place along cracks to form 'dykes', or along layers in sedimentary rocks to form 'sills'. These rocks take longer to cool and the mineral grains have time to grow larger, forming medium-grained rocks such as dolerite. Deeper in the Earth's crust, magma may accumulate in large chambers that act as feeders to volcanoes at the surface. Such bodies take a long time to solidify, forming coarse-grained rocks such as granite and gabbro.

Basalt

SEDIMENTARY ROCKS form when rocks are broken down by weathering and by the action of water, wind and ice. Fragments of rock are then transported by rivers, tides or currents, by the wind, or by glaciers and ice sheets, to be deposited as sediments in river channels, floodplains, seas, oceans, lakes, deserts or by retreating glaciers and ice sheets. These sediments may then be buried by

Limestone

Photo – Bill Bachman

succeeding layers and over time become hardened into solid rock. Rocks made up of boulders, cobbles and pebbles are called conglomerates, those made up of sand are sandstone, and those formed of silt and mud are siltstones, mudstones and shales. Sedimentary rocks also form by the accumulation of animal and plant remains, forming limestone or coal.

METAMORPHIC ROCKS are formed when igneous or sedimentary rocks are altered by heat and/or pressure: turning sandstone and mudstone into schist and gneiss; basalt into amphibolite; limestone into marble; and granite and gabbro into granitic gneiss, amphibolite and granulite. Metamorphism may occur when major earth movements bury rocks deep in the Earth's crust, or through heating next to an igneous intrusion. New minerals, such as garnet, grow as the rock recrystallises.

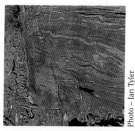

Metamorphic rock

Photo – Ian Tyler

In the Pinnacles Desert, which lies within Nambung National Park north of Perth, are the spectacular remains of a once vegetated sand dune system that formed during the last one million years.

DESCRIPTION: Thousands of huge limestone pillars rise from a stark landscape of yellow sand. Reaching up to three and a half metres tall, they form a variety of shapes, from jagged sharp-edged forms to smooth mushroom shapes.

ROCK TYPES: The pillars are made of Tamala Limestone, the same rock type that extends along most of the coastline of the South-West (see pages 20-21). It was originally quartz and lime sand, brought ashore by waves and then carried inland by the wind to form dunes during the Pleistocene. The action of the wind is preserved as cross-bedding structures in many of the pillars. The grains were then cemented together by calcium carbonate, leached from the lime sand by percolating rainwater, turning the dunes into limestone.

LANDFORM FORMATION: While the dunes were being formed, plant roots stabilised their surface and an acidic layer of soil and humus (containing decayed plant and animal matter) developed over the upper sandy layers. The acidic soil accelerated the leaching process, forming a hard layer of calcrete over the softer limestone that was forming below. Plant roots exploited cracks that formed in the calcrete layer. When water seeped down along these channels, the softer limestone was slowly leached away, leaving behind insoluble quartz sand, which also filled the channels. This subsurface erosion continued until only the most resilient columns remained. The Pinnacles are therefore the eroded remnants of a formerly thick bed of limestone.

As bush fires denuded the higher areas, south-westerly winds carried away the loose quartz sand left behind after the

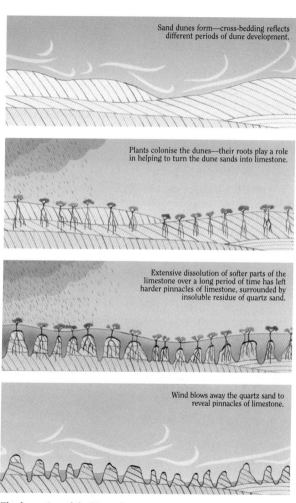

Sand dunes form—cross-bedding reflects different periods of dune development.

Plants colonise the dunes—their roots play a role in helping to turn the dune sands into limestone.

Extensive dissolution of softer parts of the limestone over a long period of time has left harder pinnacles of limestone, surrounded by insoluble residue of quartz sand.

Wind blows away the quartz sand to reveal pinnacles of limestone.

The formation of the Pinnacles

leaching, leaving limestone pillars. They were probably exposed about 6000 years ago and then covered up by shifting sands before being exposed again in the last few hundred years. This process can be seen today by the predominantly southerly winds that uncover pinnacles in the northern part of the Pinnacles Desert but cover those in the south. Other examples of pinnacles, but not as well developed, can be seen near Guilderton, Lake Gnangara, Bibra Lake and Mandurah.

NOTABLE FEATURES: Common egg-shaped structures are found in the limestone. They are fossilised pupal cases of a species of weevil. The beetle-like larvae burrowed into the sand and then secreted a case around its body in readiness for metamorphosis. The higher acidity of these cases encouraged water to dissolve and secrete cement around them. They are hollow inside and may have a hole at one end from which the adult weevil emerged. They have since been exposed by erosion.

Fossilised pupal cases of a weevil

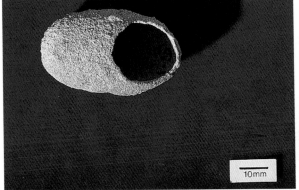

10mm

Photo - Ken McNamara

Above and below: *Pinnacles of various shapes*

A chain of limestone islands reefs and banks lie offshore from Perth. The most popular and well known of these are Rottnest and Penguin islands.

DESCRIPTION: Rottnest is the largest island, 10.5 kilometres long and up to 4.5 kilometres wide. Penguin Island is much smaller, only about 800 metres at its widest point, and lies just 700 metres off the mainland. It is surrounded by the Shoalwater Islands Marine Park. Both islands are covered with low heath and grasses, and Rottnest also has pines and wattles. Rocky limestone headlands, bays and sandy beaches surround both islands.

ROCK TYPES: The Tamala Limestone makes up most of the islands and was formed in the Pleistocene. It is composed of cemented wind-blown dune deposits of shell fragments (lime) and quartz, and is part of the Spearwood Dune System of the Swan Coastal Plain (see pages 22-25). Large cross bedding is common and marks successive dune slopes as they migrated along the coastline. The limestone has weathered to form a layer of quartz sand that now covers much of the islands' surfaces.

Limestone rich in corals and shells (gastropods) is found on Rottnest Island at Fairbridge Bluff in Salmon Bay. This is a shallow reef deposit called the Rottnest Limestone, which formed when sea level rose slightly during the time when the Tamala Limestone dunes were deposited. Shell beds known as the Herschell Limestone are present around the margins of the salt lakes on Rottnest, and contain more than 200 species of marine fauna. These were deposited when the sea level was several metres higher than today, when the salt lakes were coastal lagoons. Thin beds of lime sand, marl, peat and algal sediments are found in several swamps on Rottnest, and contain fossil pollen from a forest that once covered up to 65 per cent of the island. The trees included tuart, jarrah, marri, banksia, peppermint, sheoak and zamia palms.

Photo – Michael James

Above: *Penguin Island*   Below: *Rottnest Island*

Photo – Dennis Sarson/Lochman Transparencies

LANDFORM FORMATION: About 140 000 years ago (in the Pleistocene), during a major ice age, the sea level was about 130 metres lower than it is today. The islands offshore from Perth were all part of the Swan Coastal Plain, which was then partly covered by the Spearwood Dune System (Tamala Limestone). As the icecaps contracted again over the next 10 000 years, the sea level rose to near its present height and reefs grew at Rottnest Island (Rottnest Limestone). The sea level then began to fall again during the last ice age, reaching its lowest level some 18 000 years ago. The coastline was then about 12 kilometres west of Rottnest and the old dunes were hills high above the Swan Coastal Plain.

When the sea level rapidly rose again, as the icecaps began to contract for the last time, dunes again developed over the plain, forming several ridges that linked the islands to the mainland. The islands were separated from the mainland about 6500 years ago, and this resulted in major changes in the plants and animals. With the higher sea level a new era of dune building began, known as the Quindalup Dune System. Sand was swept across the newly drowned coastal plain and washed ashore. In addition, the south-westerly winds and waves eroded the offshore ridges, further reducing their size, forming a chain of islands and reefs such as Penguin Island, Seal Island, Bird Island and Peron Peninsula. Where the coast was sheltered by an island or shallow reef, the force of the waves was reduced and sediment was preferentially deposited between them. A triangular spit built out from the mainland towards the adjacent island, forming a low promontory consisting of line after line of low parallel dunes. The land surrounding Rockingham is made up of such a landform. Point Peron was once an offshore island but was 'captured' by the advancing growth of dunes.

About 6000 years ago, the sea rose about two and half

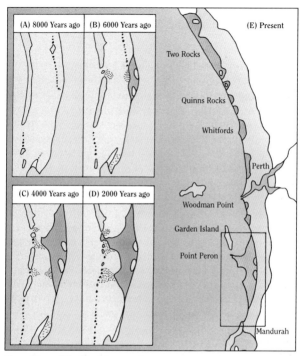

Formation of Rockingham coast

metres above today's level. This resulted in the flooding of large parts of Rottnest, creating more than 10 separate islands and the deposition of shell beds in lagoons (Herschell Limestone). Since then, the sea level has fallen to its present position.

NOTABLE FEATURES: Along the headlands of Rottnest and Penguin Islands are prominent platforms and notches high up within the limestone. These mark successive sea-level changes during the Pleistocene and Holocene, when waves eroded ancient headlands, similar to what's happening today.

Creamy white limestone cliffs are a conspicuous feature of much of the South-West's coastline and the islands near to Perth.

DESCRIPTION: Present as cliffs and headlands along popular beaches such as Cottesloe and Rockingham, and forming magnificent cliffs in D'Entrecasteaux National Park, the limestone also extends offshore as reefs, rock flats and islands. At Yanchep and Leeuwin-Naturaliste national parks, caves have formed in this coastal limestone (see pages 44-45).

ROCK TYPES: The limestone contains a high proportion of lime sand derived from sea shells and minute marine organisms, and is known as the Tamala Limestone. During the early years of the Swan River Colony, this limestone was quarried to supply the colony's early building needs, and can be seen in many of the old buildings and homes around Perth and Fremantle, for example, at Fremantle Prison and the University of Western Australia. It is now quarried mostly for cement production from small mines along the coast in the Perth Metropolitan Region.

LANDFORM FORMATION: The Tamala Limestone formed as sand dunes and beach deposits during the last one million years. This was during the Pleistocene when the sea level changed dramatically in response to the expansion and contraction of the polar iceaps. The lime sand was slowly dissolved by rainwater, then deposited again when the water evaporated, cementing the sand grains together and turning the dunes into limestone. In many places you can see obvious cross bedding, which is evidence of its origin as wind-blown sand dunes. The thin strata are inclined at various oblique angles, often set abruptly against other strata, reflecting the original pattern of sand accumulation and changes in wind action. The direction in which the wind blew can be determined from the shape of the dunes. This cross bedding can also commonly be seen in the building stones. Along the Leeuwin-

Limestone cliffs around Eagle Bay at Rottnest Island

Naturaliste coastline and around to Esperance, the dunes can be seen covering granite and gneiss.

NOTABLE FEATURES: Masses of tubular structures are common within the limestone. These are fossilised roots, or 'rhizoliths' of plants and trees that once inhabited the dunes. They form when the roots decay and the space left is filled with lime sand and cement from the dissolved sand. When the surrounding limestone is weathered, their shape is preserved.

SWAN COASTAL PLAIN

Millions of years ago, when Australia was part of the ancient continent of Gondwana, a large fault formed along what is now the Darling Scarp. As the fault moved over time, the area to the west formed a huge sedimentary basin, the Perth Basin, which filled up with an incredible 15 kilometres of marine and river sediments. A veneer of soil and sand and a variety of distinctive landforms now overlie part of this basin, forming what is now known as the Swan Coastal Plain. Much of Perth's water supply is pumped from these sandy deposits.

DESCRIPTION: This low-lying, gently undulating area lies between the Darling Scarp and the coast, and extends from Geraldton to Dunsborough. The most easterly landform is an old scree slope that runs along the front of the scarp, forming the foothills. An alluvial plain lies in front of this, and to the west lies a series of sand dunes, including prominent coastal exposures of the Tamala Limestone. Several rivers such as the Moore River, Swan River, Murray River and Collie River, drain from the Darling Plateau and cross the plain.

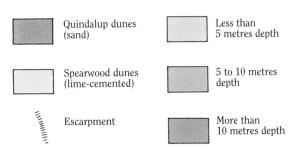

Quindalup dunes (sand)

Less than 5 metres depth

Spearwood dunes (lime-cemented)

5 to 10 metres depth

Escarpment

More than 10 metres depth

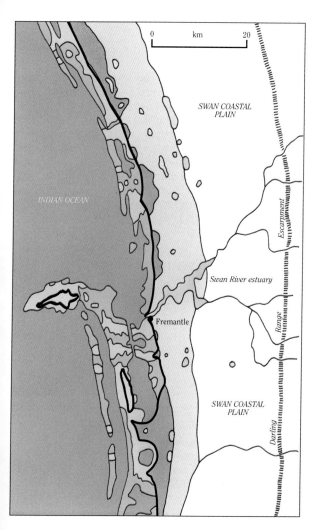

SWAN COASTAL PLAIN

INDIAN OCEAN

Swan River estuary

Fremantle

SWAN COASTAL PLAIN

Escarpment

Range

Darling

0 km 20

23

ROCK TYPES: Most of the Swan Coastal Plain consists of quartz and lime sand formed by wind-blown dunes known as the Bassendean, Spearwood, and Quindalup Dune Systems. Some of this sand is quarried in the Perth Metropolitan Region for use in glass making and cement manufacture. Mining of very high quality quartz sand also takes place at Kemerton near Bunbury. The Tamala Limestone is part of the Spearwood Dune System and is the main rock type on the Swan Coastal Plain. It forms distinctive coastal cliffs and larger hills such as Kings Park (see pages 20-21). Clays and loamy soils of the Pinjarra Plain form close to the Darling Scarp, transported mostly from the Darling Plateau by rivers and streams. The clays are used to make tiles and bricks and the loamy soils grow the vineyards of the Swan River Valley.

LANDFORM FORMATION: For about the last two to three million years, during the Pliocene and Pleistocene eras, the polar icecaps have repeatedly contracted and expanded making the sea level rise and fall. This has sculpted the Swan Coastal Plain to the way we see it today. In the Pliocene the Darling Range was a ridge of low cliffs and the sea lapped at its base. The sands deposited along this ancient shoreline are today part of Perth's foothills. During the next few hundred thousand years, the sea level dropped and the shoreline moved westward. Rivers and creeks from the Darling Range emptied sand and silt onto the newly formed Pinjarra Plain and sand dunes of the Bassendean Dune System formed along the coastal plain.

About one million years ago, a new era of dune building began, forming the Spearwood Dune System, which partly covered the previous dunes and slowly turned to limestone. During this time, in the last ice age, the sea level dropped to 130 metres below its present level, with the shoreline lying west of Rottnest Island. The Swan River was forced to cut down into the

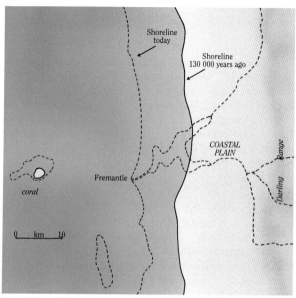

Swan Coastal Plain - past sea levels

coastal plain, forming the cliffs of Tamala Limestone now seen at Kings Park, Blackwall Reach and around the river mouth at Fremantle. It also formed a new section of river north of Rottnest, which today is a submarine canyon known as the Perth Canyon. Since then the sea has risen to its present level, flooding the coast and forming sand dunes, bars and spits along the coast. These are now part of the Quindalup Dune System.

NOTABLE FEATURES: The undulating hills that parallel the shoreline in many coastal suburbs, like Fremantle, are ancient dunes. They record the positions of successive coastlines during the last million years. Many swamps and lakes have formed within depressions between these dune systems, such as at Yalgorup National Park (see pages 34-35).

East of Perth, a line of eucalypt-covered hills known as the Darling Range extends for about 300 kilometres from near Dandaragan to the east of Bunbury. These hills are made of rocks that are up to a staggering 3700 million years old, in stark contrast to the very young sand dunes of the Swan Coastal Plain to the west. The range is at the south-western edge of the Yilgarn Craton that formed as part of an ancient continent more than 2400 million years ago.

DESCRIPTION: The western edge of the Darling Range is called the Darling Scarp, which is the surface expression of an extensive geological structure known as the Darling Fault. The scarp rises steeply to more than 200 metres above sea level, where it flattens out to form the Darling Plateau. This is a vast, gently undulating area of mostly eucalypt-covered hills and broad deep valleys, dissected by rivers and streams and rising to nearly 600 metres above sea level.

ROCK TYPES: The main rock types are varieties of granite and gneiss that formed between about 3700 and 2650 million years ago. They contain mostly quartz, feldspar and biotite mica. Fresh granite and gneiss are quarried in several places in the range for road-base material. When the granite weathers, the feldspar and mica form a white clay called kaolin. This white mottling can often be seen in road cuttings in the hills. Along the Darling Fault are rocks that have been highly flattened and stretched, known as 'mylonite'. These formed when the fault moved, shearing and grinding the rocks under extreme pressure. Dolerite has intruded the granite and gneiss in many places, commonly forming thick vertical bodies, or dykes. When fresh, the dolerite is black or dark grey and is commonly known as 'black granite', a sought-after building stone. When it weathers it produces a very red soil because of its high iron content. Migmatite (literally 'mixed rock')

Above: *Looking from the Darling Scarp to the Swan Coastal Plain*
Below: *Granite and gneiss up to 3700 million years old*

Photo – Len Stewart/Lochman Transparencies

Photo – Dennis Sarson/Lochman Transparencies

can be found around the Canning and Serpentine Dams. This formed when earlier gneissic rocks were intruded by granites, melting some of the gneiss and leaving other areas that didn't quite reach its melting point. Near Boddington, there are also some volcanic rocks that formed nearly 2700 million years ago.

A hard red capping that looks like cemented gravel, called duricrust, overlies the Darling Plateau. Where it is weathered, it forms the distinctive 'pea-gravel' used in roads and pathways. The duricrust, together with mottled soils and clay that it overlies, is called laterite. Near Pinjarra and Boddington, laterite is mined for aluminium and gold (see pages 30-31).

LANDFORM FORMATION: The Darling Range was formed by movement of the Darling Fault; its eastern side (Darling Plateau) moved upwards and its western side (Swan Coastal Plain) moved downwards. It has probably existed as some form of upland for at least 290 million years. However, it would not have always looked as it does today. It would not have been as continuous or as high, with part of the shoreline sometimes being well inland on the Darling Plateau. About 40 million years ago, during the Eocene, Western Australia's climate was quite tropical. These conditions were ideal for the formation of duricrust, which now caps much of the plateau. Around two or three million years ago, the Darling Scarp formed low coastal cliffs when the sea level was substantially higher than it is today. The shoreline sands that were deposited along its base may in places contain mineral sands, some of which have been mined near Capel (see pages 40-41).

NOTABLE FEATURES: The Darling Fault forms an almost straight line for about 1000 kilometres from the south coast, just near Point D'Entrecasteaux, up to east of Shark Bay, and is a major structure within the Earth's crust. It was first formed well over 2500 million years ago during the Archaean, and continued to be

The Darling Scarp has formed along the Darling Fault

very active up to about 135 million years ago, when Australia split from Greater India. Between 430 and 135 million years ago (Silurian to Cretaceous), the western side of the Darling Fault repeatedly dropped, allowing that area to fill up with river and marine sediments. Up to 15 kilometres of sedimentary rock, known as the Perth Basin, now underlies the Swan Coastal Plain. The fault has moved during the past 135 million years, although not substantially.

Large deposits of aluminium and gold are contained in laterite in the Boddington-Pinjarra area of the Darling Range. Aluminium was first discovered here at the turn of the twentieth century, but mining did not commence until 1963. Now, the Huntly-Del Park, Willowdale and Mount Saddleback opencut mines form the richest aluminium-producing region in the world. The aluminium ore is transported to refineries at Collie, Kwinana, Pinjarra and Wagerup for processing into aluminium metal. The laterite also contains gold near Boddington, first detected by the Geological Survey of Western Australia in 1979. In 1987 this area was developed into a mine, and it is now the second largest producer of gold in Australia. Gold was also mined at the nearby, but much smaller, Hedges mine (now closed).

ROCK TYPES: Laterite forms a blanket over much of the Darling Plateau. It consists of mottled soils and clays overlain by a distinctive hard red-brown cap called duricrust. Where the laterite is aluminium-rich, commonly containing the mineral gibbsite, it is called bauxite. At Boddington, gold is also found in the laterite (as very small dispersed grains), as well as in the underlying volcanic rocks of the 2700-million-year-old Saddleback Group.

FORMATION AND DISTINCTIVE GEOLOGICAL FEATURES: Laterite forms during extended periods when there are distinct wet and dry seasons, typically in tropical climates. During the wet season, rain gradually leaches out the more soluble elements, such as sodium, magnesium, potassium and calcium, from the rocks. During the dry season, these were drawn to the surface as salts, where they were washed away with the next rains, leaving behind deposits rich in insoluble iron and aluminium oxides. Over time, a thick zone of clay and mottled soil develops over the weathering rocks, and a hard red capping of duricrust forms at the surface, a common feature throughout the South-West. Together, this

Soils and clay overlain by duricrust

mixture is called laterite. In the Darling Plateau, tropical conditions began to develop about 40 million years ago (during the Eocene) and laterite formed from deep weathering of the igneous and metamorphic rocks. Aluminium was concentrated as bauxite lenses, and at Boddington gold was concentrated in the laterite that formed over gold-rich volcanic rocks.

Along the Albany Highway, just past Armadale, several conspicuous granite hills rise out of forests rich in eucalypts and banksias. These are the Monadnocks, consisting of Eagle Hill, Mount Randall, Mount Cuthbert, Mount Vincent, and Mount Cooke. They form part of the Monadnocks Conservation Park and can easily be accessed via the Bibbulmun Track.

DESCRIPTION: Large rounded 'bald' hills reach up to 582 metres above sea level, the highest point of the Darling Plateau. These hills form the divide between the Canning and Serpentine drainage systems. Monadnock is a term used by geologists to describe large isolated hills that stand above a generally flat plain. The hills have a peculiar 'humpback' shape. Large areas of lichen and moss commonly cover these rocky hills, and around them are broad valleys traversed by creeks and rivers.

ROCK TYPES: The Monadnocks consist of granite that formed around 2650 million years ago, from magma (molten rock) that started to crystallise about 14 kilometres below the Earth's surface. The rock is mostly coarse grained and comprises quartz, feldspar, biotite mica and some hornblende. Around Mount Cuthbert and Mount Vincent, the rock contains large crystals of feldspar and is called porphyritic granite. This texture is thought to form when magma moved from deep in the Earth's crust, where it was cooling slowly and growing large crystals, to a higher level in the crust, where it cooled more rapidly. As a result, the remaining liquid formed smaller crystals. Thin white veins of quartz are commonly found throughout the granite. These formed when hot fluids rich in silica travelled along fractures within the newly formed granite.

LANDFORM FORMATION: The Monadnocks are part of a much larger granite body called the Darling Range Batholith. It forms a triangular shape, extending from near New Norcia down to near Bridgetown and eastwards towards the Stirling Range. The

A climber on Mount Cuthbert

unusual isolated nature of the Monadnocks is probably due to the area having very widely spaced joints and fractures compared with the surrounding rocks. As the granite is weathered, these widely spaced joints result in huge single blocks of granite being preferentially preserved.

NOTABLE FEATURES: Large slabs of granite are commonly scattered over the hills and around their sides. This type of 'onion peeling' forms by a combination of continual heating and cooling of the rock's surface, called physical weathering, and moisture in cracks, called chemical weathering. Mosses and lichens also break down the surface, but at a much slower rate.

Yalgorup National Park, on the western edge of the Swan Coastal Plain just south of the Dawesville Channel near Mandurah, covers a chain of 10 narrow lakes. This distinctive landform is famous for its rock-like structures, known as thrombolites, on the edge of Lake Clifton.

DESCRIPTION: The lake system is about 43 kilometres long and four kilometres wide, and forms three distinct depressions that parallel the coast. Lake Preston is extremely elongated and is the closest to the coast. Behind this is a series of discontinuous lakes comprising (from north to south): Swan Pond, Duck Pond, Boundary Lake, Lake Pollard, Martins Tank Lake, Lake Yalgorup, Lake Hayward and Newnham Lake. Lake Clifton is the furthest from the coast and the nearest to the Old Coast Road and is extremely elongated.

ROCK TYPES: The lakes lie within the Spearwood Dune System, a series of Pleistocene dunes that covered much of the Swan Coastal Plain when the sea level was substantially lower than it is today. These were slowly transformed to limestone, known as the Tamala Limestone, which forms cliffs along much of the South-West coast (see pages 20-21). Quartz and shell fragments make up the limestone and the loose dune sand.

LANDFORM FORMATION: During the last one million years, the sea level has periodically risen and fallen as the polar icecaps have contracted and expanded. The position of the coastline subsequently shifted both eastward, as the sea level rose, and westward, as the sea level fell. In its wake a series of coastal sand dunes formed, some of which were later swept away when the sea covered them. These sandy deposits became the Spearwood Dune System. Those dunes that remained became fossilised, turning to limestone by percolating rainwater that cemented the grains together (see pages 12-13). When the sea level rose after the last ice age so did the water

Thrombolites at Lake Clifton

table underlying the coastal plain, forming the Yalgorup lake system in the depressions between the dunes. Over the last 10 000 years, sand has been blown in from the coast or washed ashore to form the Quindalup Dune System, which is superimposed over the old dunes for up to two kilometres from the beach.

NOTABLE FEATURES: Rock-like structures known as thrombolites can be seen on the eastern edge of Lake Clifton. Like the famous stromatolites of Hamelin Pool Marine Nature Reserve in Shark Bay, the thrombolites are built by micro-organisms, which have population densities of 3000 per square metre. Lake Clifton is one of only a few places in Western Australia with living thrombolites. The lake contains upwellings of fresh groundwater that are high in calcium carbonate (or lime). The micro-organisms living in this shallow lake are able to precipitate calcium carbonate from the water during photosynthesis, forming the mineralised structure that is the thrombolite.

The Collie Basin east of Bunbury is Western Australia's only producing coalfield, and contains the State's main coal reserves. This coal is used to generate about 80 per cent of Western Australia's electricity needs. Coal fragments were first discovered in the bed of the Collie River in 1883, and exploration and mining followed in 1898. There are currently four opencut mines and three underground mines, containing a massive 2400 million tonnes of coal. The mines have 60 main coal seams that can reach 13 metres thick. The rocks are of Permian age (280 million years old) and form beds that dip towards the south-west.

ROCK TYPES: The coal is interbedded with siltstone and sandstone, giving the faces in the opencut mines a distinct banded look. Below the coal seams are rocks that contain pebbles and cobbles of dolerite, quartzite, and granite. This is known as tillite, deposited when glaciers moved over a landscape of igneous and metamorphic rocks, breaking them away and grinding them up from the valley floors and walls. A thick blanket of sand, gravel and duricrust now forms an undulating landscape over the basin.

FORMATION AND DISTINCTIVE GEOLOGICAL FEATURES: Most of Western Australia was covered by glaciers about 280 million years ago during the Permian. At that time, Australia was part of Gondwana and close to the South Pole. As it drifted slowly northwards, the ice melted, leaving thick beds of tillite. Twenty million years later a warmer climate encouraged swamps and forests to develop over large parts of the South-West. The ancient sediments in the swamps were rich in rotting organic material, which were compressed by the weight of up to eight kilometres of sediments that accumulated above them over the following millions of years. This pressure slowly turned them into coal. Fossil leaves and plant spores have been found in the coal-bearing strata, including those of *Glossopteris*, an extinct plant also found

Imprints of Glossopteris *leaves from middle to late Permian rocks at Collie's Muja opencut mine*

in other remnants of Gondwana, such as India and South Africa. Most of the Permian rocks were eventually weathered and eroded away, but around Collie they were preserved in the small, sunken Collie Basin.

BUNBURY BASALT

The results of an ancient volcanic eruption, believed to have occurred about 135 million years ago, can be seen in the South-West. It is thought that during this time, flows of molten lava erupted from fissures located offshore from south-western Australia, and spread out in a belt more than 275 kilometres long. They poured out during the rupturing of the crust that accompanied the break-up of Gondwana during the Cretaceous period, as the Indian Ocean was beginning to form.

DESCRIPTION: The only outcrops of Bunbury Basalt can be seen at the northern end of Ocean Beach in Bunbury and at Black Point in D'Entrecasteaux National Park, south-east of Augusta. The basalt at Bunbury is fairly unspectacular but nonetheless fascinating and, being close to a road, easy to see. It formed a flow about two kilometres long and 100 metres wide. The hexagonal columns at Black Point, however, are stunning, even more so as they are constantly buffeted by waves of the Southern Ocean. Access to this remote area is by four-wheel drive only.

ROCK TYPES: Basalt is a dark fine-grained rock of volcanic origin. The main minerals include pyroxene, hornblende and feldspar. Basalt, commonly called 'blue metal', is used extensively in road building. In the South-West it is quarried at Gelorup, south of Bunbury, for building, construction and road material.

LANDFORM FORMATION: Basalt was formed from the fast cooling of a lava flow. As it cooled the rock shrank, causing a close-packed series of hexagonal columns to form, similar to the way mud cracks develop. These structures are very similar to those of the well-known Giant's Causeway in Northern Ireland. The sea is now slowly eroding the basalt.

NOTABLE FEATURES: On the beach at Bunbury, numerous holes called 'vesicles' can still be seen in the basalt. The vesicles represent gas bubbles trapped in the lava as it cooled.

Above: *Basalt at Bunbury*   Below: *Basalt columns at Black Point*

In the late 1940s, exploration for sand rich in minerals (ilmenite and zircon) began along modern beaches in the Capel-Bunbury area. Economic deposits were eventually found during the early 1950s in fossil shorelines about seven kilometres inland near Capel, deposited when the sea level was much higher. Mining commenced in 1956, and today nearly one million tonnes of ilmenite and 100 000 tonnes of zircon are produced each year, helping to make Western Australia a major world supplier of mineral sands. The titanium contained in ilmenite is used extensively in making the white pigment for paint, paper and plastics.

DESCRIPTION: The mineral sands form beds within low hills of quartz sand that are part of the Bassendean, Spearwood and Quindalup Dune Systems (see page 24). They mostly contain the fine-grained minerals ilmenite and zircon, which may make up to 90 per cent of the fossil shoreline sands. Many of the dunes that have been mined have now been rehabilitated as either small wetlands or farmland.

FORMATION AND DISTINCTIVE GEOLOGICAL FEATURES: The minerals that are now found in the sands were probably originally widely dispersed within sedimentary, igneous and metamorphic rocks inland from Capel. Weathering resulted in the minerals being eroded from the rocks and then transported by rivers and streams over the Swan Coastal Plain. As the sea level rose during the Pleistocene, the minerals, being heavier than the quartz and lime sand, were concentrated by waves along the ancient shorelines. More than 10 such shorelines have been discovered. Capel was near to the coastline during part of this time, with at least four shorelines preserved nearby that record when the sea level was slightly higher or lower than at present. These shorelines have also been mined for their mineral sands.

Above: *Mininnup Beach before mining* Below: *Layers of mineral sands*

The Greenbushes mine, about 80 kilometres south-east of Bunbury, is the world's largest producer of tantalum and lithium. A mass of pegmatite veins, about 3.3 kilometres long and up to 250 metres wide, contain the mineral deposit. Mining began in alluvial deposits within creeks, and later moved to the weathered pegmatite. Today, fresh pegmatite is mined from two large opencut pits that have a life of up to 25 years. Mining began in 1888, when tin, as the mineral cassiterite, was discovered in alluvial deposits associated with the pegmatite. It is now mainly a by-product to the much more profitable tantalum and lithium. Tantalum, as the mineral tantalite, was discovered in 1893, but it wasn't until the 1970s that it became profitable to mine. It is now used extensively in the electronics industry. In 1949, spodumene, the major lithium mineral, was identified in the pegmatite by the Geological Survey of Western Australia. During the late 1970s, a large deposit of the mineral was discovered, which is now used in glass and ceramic production and television components.

ROCK TYPES: Pegmatite is a very coarse-grained variety of granite that crystallised from granitic magma. At Greenbushes it is rich in different minerals including spodumene, cassiterite, tantalite, uranite, microlite, feldspar, quartz, mica, beryl, tourmaline and garnet. Deep weathering of the pegmatite has also produced high quality kaolin clay, used for making ceramics. The surrounding country rock, into which the pegmatite intruded, consists of gneiss, amphibolite and schist. These contain mostly quartz, feldspar, mica and amphiboles.

FORMATION AND DISTINCTIVE GEOLOGICAL FEATURES: About 2530 million years ago, the crust around Greenbushes underwent an extreme amount of stress. As a result, a roughly north-south zone of weakness formed within the country rock, 150 kilometres long and 20 kilometres wide, known as the Donnybrook-Bridgetown

Top: *Tantalum pit showing tantalite/tin bearing pegmatite*

Above: *Tantalum product*
Right: *Tin ingots*

Shear Zone. Magma intruded this zone, cooling to form granite and pegmatite, with tantalum, lithium and tin concentrated in some of the pegmatite's minerals.

Along the coastline of the Leeuwin-Naturaliste National Park, limestone cliffs are riddled with shallow caves and ledges that open to the sea. Inland, however, similar caves form extensive subterranean networks. Many limestone caves have been recorded in the park, several of which are open to tourists, such as Giants Cave, Calgardup Cave, Lake Cave and Mammoth Cave.

DESCRIPTION: The caves form a labyrinth of tunnels and shafts, some containing streams and pools, and are connected to the surface through openings in the forests and heath. In some places, large depressions in the landscape mark collapsed caves.

ROCK TYPES: The caves have developed in the Tamala Limestone, which consists of quartz and lime sand (calcium carbonate). It was deposited during the Pleistocene as wind-blown dunes, when the sea level was up to 130 metres lower than it is today. Soon after the dunes formed, the grains were bound together when percolating rainwater dissolved some of the lime, reprecipitating it as cement.

LANDFORM FORMATION: The caves were formed when weak acids slowly dissolved the underlying limestone. These acids were produced by the mixing of rainwater with dissolved carbon dioxide from the atmosphere and from decaying vegetation at the soil surface. The acid solution enlarged cracks and other lines of weakness such as old tree root tunnels. Once cavities began to form in the limestone, streams and rivers and underground lakes fed by groundwater and surface run-off developed, further enlarging the passages and chambers and connecting them to form a cave network.

NOTABLE FEATURES: Speleothems (cave decorations) are formed when the dissolved calcium carbonate is redeposited from solution, similar to the way that the cement binding the Tamala Limestone is formed. In this case, however, there is nothing for it

Stalactites and flowstone formations at Giants Cave

Photo – Brett Dennis/Lochman Tranparencies

to bind to, so it grows into open cavities forming various shapes. Speleothems range from minute helictites, only a few millimetres long, to large pillars and flowstones, weighing several tonnes. There are also stalactites, stalagmites, shawls, columns and straws.

Animals sometimes fell or were trapped inside the caves. Their bones have been preserved, many from animals that have long been extinct in Western Australia, such as the thylacine (Tasmanian tiger), Tasmanian devil and koala. There are also bones from giant marsupials or 'megafauna', including a wombat, wallaby and echidna, all of which are now extinct. The giant wombat (*Phascolonus gigas*) was possibly the largest burrowing marsupial ever to have lived, being about twice the size of a modern wombat.

SUGARLOAF ROCK AND CANAL ROCKS

Sugarloaf Rock and Canal Rocks lie just offshore from the northern end of Leeuwin Naturaliste National Park. They are good examples of the Leeuwin Complex, a highly deformed and metamorphosed group of rocks that underlie much of the anvil-shaped promontory along which Caves Road runs. These rocks were part of a mountain belt that formed along the lower west coast of Western Australia about 1100 million years ago.

ROCK TYPES: Sugarloaf Rock and Canal Rocks are composed of granitic gneiss which outcrops all along this coastline. The gneiss was originally granite and pegmatite (veins of mostly coarse-grained feldspar and quartz) that formed between 1100 and 530 million years ago, possibly when the Western Australian Craton collided with a similar craton that lay to the west. Enormous temperatures and pressures were generated as the continents collided, metamorphosing the granite to gneiss.

LANDFORM FORMATION: Relatively recent weathering by pounding waves, sea spray and slow erosion by marine organisms has stripped off much of the limestone along the Leeuwin-Naturaliste coast, leaving the underlying granitic gneiss. The canal at Canal Rocks follows a fault that has been preferentially weathered and eroded by waves and currents. Likewise, fractures and joints that surround Sugarloaf Rock have probably also controlled how the rock weathered into its unusual shape.

NOTABLE FEATURES: Close inspection of these rocks reveals thin bands of alternating dark and light minerals. The lighter minerals are feldspar and quartz, and the darker minerals are pyroxene, hornblende and garnet. The bands formed when the original granite was metamorphosed and deformed under high temperatures of almost 700°C and pressures approximately 5000 times that of atmospheric pressure. This resulted in melting of parts of the rock, recrystallisation, and then separation of minerals rich in silica and

Photo – Geoff Taylor/Lochman Transparencies

Above: *Canal Rocks*   Below: *Sugarloaf Rock*

Photo – John Green

aluminium from those rich in iron and magnesium. Sharply curved bands, called shear zones, are common throughout the rocks, and indicate areas where the granitic gneiss has been subject to extreme stress. In places, the banding may be very thin and drawn out, whereas in others it may form drawn out 'sausage' shapes, a process known as boudinage. This variation in band shape and size resulted when the rock was stretched somewhat like plasticine, when the crust underwent enormous tensional forces.

Some of the South-West's most stunning coastline stretches between Walpole and Mount Manypeaks, for example, at William Bay National Park, West Cape Howe National Park and Torndirrup National Park near Albany. For more than 140 kilometres, windswept coastal heaths give way to massive granite outcrops, sheer cliffs, and steep sandy slopes and dunes. Most of the rocks belong to the Nornalup Complex, part of the eroded roots of a mountain chain formed when two ancient continents collided.

DESCRIPTION: The coastline consists of grey, sheer cliffs and boulder-strewn headlands that form a series of spectacular bays and peninsulas. At Torndirrup National Park, the Southern Ocean has sculpted a 'Natural Bridge' in the coastal granites and gneisses. Nearby are 'The Gap', where huge waves rush in and out with tremendous ferocity, and 'The Blowholes' where water and air rush up joints in the rock, spraying the surrounding area.

ROCK TYPES: The Nornalup Complex along the coast consists of granite, granodiorite, gneiss and migmatite. These rocks contain the minerals quartz, feldspar, biotite mica, garnet and hornblende. The oldest rock is gneiss. This is recognised by its banded pattern of different coloured mineral layers. Mount Martin, just east of Albany, consists of gneiss with large eye-shaped 'clots' of biotite mica and very large crystals of feldspar. This variety is called augen gneiss. It forms when porphyritic granite (granite with large scattered crystals) is subject to the high temperatures and pressures of metamorphism. The gneiss along the coast was originally granite that formed around 1450 million years ago. It was then transformed, or metamorphosed, under extremely high pressures and temperatures to gneiss about 150 million years later.

Granite, which intruded as magma around 1180 million years ago, is the dominant rock type along the coastline.

Above: *West Cape Howe* Below: *Natural Bridge, Torndirrup*

Photo – Gordon Roberts

Photo – Gordon Roberts

49

It squeezed into the gneiss and formed several very large bodies, or batholiths, some of which are now exposed at William Bay, Mount Clarence in Albany, Stony Hill in Torndirrup National Park and at Mount Manypeaks. This rock type is recognised by its large crystals and the rounded shape of its weathered boulders. Large pieces, or xenoliths, of gneiss are found within the granite, having been broken off from the hard gneiss in which it intruded. At The Gap, you can see the complex association formed when the granite magma intruded into, and mixed with, the much older gneiss.

Around Whaling Cove, in Torndirrup National Park, migmatite is the main rock type. This formed when the granite intruded into the gneiss and partly melted it. At West Cape Howe, very dark grey to black rocks form the western part of the peninsula. This is dolerite, formed by injection of magma along vertical cracks or joints within the granite. It is a medium-grained rock and contains the minerals pyroxene and feldspar. Limestone, less than a million years old, is also commonly seen along the coast and is recognised by its pale colour. It overlies the other rocks and its surface is jagged as a result of weathering. Fossil shells can be found in the limestone at some sites.

LANDFORM FORMATION: Although the rocks exposed along this part of the south coast are extremely old, the landforms are relatively young. When Australia and Antarctica parted, around 120 million years ago, the sea slowly entered the rift between them and began to shape the coast. The granite and gneiss were exposed by uplift of the hinterland and by weathering and erosion of rocks that lay over them. During the last several million years, as the sea level has risen and fallen, the relentless action of waves has resulted in a series of bays and peninsulas. Joints and fractures within the rocks, and the way that the different rock types weathered, produced many of the unusual landforms along the

West Cape Howe

Photo – Tony Tapper

coast. For example, waves selectively removed fractured blocks that were less well attached to the coast, leading to the formation of features such as The Gap, The Natural Bridge and Jimmy Newhills Harbour. The sea only settled at its current level 6500 years ago. In the process it flooded river valleys, which became Albany's harbours, and created the coastline we see today.

NOTABLE FEATURES: The granites and gneisses along this coastline form part of the Nornalup Complex. This strip of rocks extends from near Point D'Entrecasteaux to Cape Riche, and northwards to Mt Frankland and the Porongurup Range (see pages 56-57). The complex is part of the eroded mountain belt known as the Albany-Fraser Orogen, which formed when the Western Australian Craton collided with the Mawson Craton between 1345 and 1140 million years ago. Similar rocks are also found at Cape Le Grand National Park.

The Stirling Range, in the Stirling Range National Park, stretches for 65 kilometres from east to west, forming a magnificent series of peaks which are the only real mountains in the South-West. The range formed when part of the Earth's crust buckled more than 500 million years ago.

DESCRIPTION: More than 20 isolated peaks form this rugged range, which reaches up to 1096 metres above sea level. They are separated by rivers, creeks and valleys, and are surrounded by aprons of gravel, sand and soil. A variety of landforms make up the Stirling Range, including peaks, foothills, large valleys, alluvial plains and wetlands. These help to influence the type of soil that forms and the amount of water available for its 1500 species of plants, including 82 species found nowhere else in the world.

ROCK TYPES: Unlike the granitic and gneissic landforms elsewhere along the southern coast, the range is composed mainly of sandstone, slate and phyllite, grouped together to form the Stirling Range Formation. The sandstone consists mostly of quartz and some feldspar and rock fragments. Some of it has been metamorphosed to form a much harder rock type called quartzite. Slate and phyllite are metamorphic rocks that were formerly sedimentary rocks, like mudstone and siltstone, rich in clay and silt. They now consist mostly of fine-grained mica and can be split into thin sheets and slabs.

The original sediments were deposited about 590 million years ago in a basin well to the south of the Stirling Range's present position. These sediments, which had been compacted and slowly turned to rock, were then thrust northwards as a thick slice over the much older granites and gneisses, similar to the manner in which the Barren Ranges were formed (see pages 60-63). The northern and southern boundaries of the range are essentially the top and bottom faults of this thrust slice. This movement took

Above: *Bluff Knoll*   Below: *Ripple marks on Toolbrunup Peak*

Photos – Jiri Lochman

place at a relatively high level in the Earth's crust; the rocks were folded, faulted and metamorphosed under much less extreme conditions than those forming gneiss. Some of these folds are very prominent on the slopes of Mondurup Peak and on the northern slope of Coyanarup Peak, where severely contorted beds wrap around through almost 180°. White veins of quartz that formed from silica-rich fluids, squeezed into open fractures within the deforming rocks.

LANDFORM FORMATION: Although the Stirling Range would have been impressive when it formed more than 500 million years ago, weathering and erosion should have levelled it off by now. Its prominence above the flat landscape is probably the result of further uplift during more recent geological times, when Australia separated from Antarctica. The distinctive shape of the Stirling Range is very much controlled by the way that the different rock types weather and the pattern of fractures that cover it. Although the three rock types are interbedded with each other, the uppermost part of the range consists mostly of sandstone and quartzite, which weathers more slowly than the slate and phyllite that is more common in the lower part. This results in many of the peaks forming sheer bluffs, such as Bluff Knoll. Blankets of eroded rocks, sand and mud, known as colluvium, form scree slopes along the range, such as at Toolbrunup Peak. This material has buried much of the rock outcrop at the base of the range, forming alluvial fans and wetlands where water has seeped out from the slopes onto the flat low-lying areas.

Ever since the Stirling Range was uplifted it has been subjected to weathering and erosion, gradually softening its features to the landforms we see today. Fracture and fault patterns within the range control these processes, resulting in the distinctive shape of hills and peaks, the orientation of cliffs, bluffs,

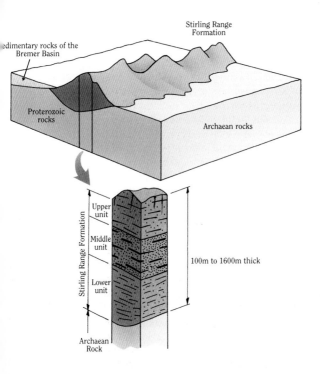

rock faces and clefts in the rocks and the location of rivers, creeks and smaller valleys.

NOTABLE FEATURES: The Stirling Range Formation was originally laid down as sand, silt and clay in rivers, tidal flats and shallow marine environments. Evidence of water movement is now preserved as ripples and mud cracks, commonly found in flat slabs of sandstone and quartzite near the summit of some peaks, such as Toolbrunup Peak and Bluff Knoll. The repetition of these ripple beds on top of each other forms exceptional examples of cross bedding.

The Porongurup Range, in the Porongurup National Park 40 kilometres north of Albany, rises some 670 metres above sea level and is renowned for its beauty and rugged terrain. This remarkable landform was formed when the Western Australian Craton collided with the Mawson Craton between 1345 and 1140 million years ago. This produced vast amounts of magma deep in the Earth's crust, which squeezed into the surrounding rocks to form massive intrusions, or batholiths. This rock is known as the Esperance Granite. Other distinctive batholiths of Esperance Granite lie along the southern coastline between Walpole and Mount Manypeaks (see pages 48-51).

DESCRIPTION: This spectacular range stretches for about 12 kilometres east to west, an island of granite standing above the surrounding flat countryside. In fact, the granite hills of the Porongurup Range were probably true islands about 40 million years ago, during the Eocene, when warm seas covered most of the coastal inland area, with the Stirling Range forming coastal cliffs.

ROCK TYPES: Granite is distinguished by its rounded boulders, and contains the minerals quartz, feldspar, biotite mica, garnet and hornblende. Large crystals of feldspar, called phenocrysts, are present throughout the rock, which is referred to as porphyritic granite. The lower slopes of the range are covered with duricrust, a remnant of a once widespread surface that began to form across the South-West during the Eocene (see page 30). Colluvium (material eroded from a higher area and accumulated lower down as scree slopes) of sand, silt, weathered granite and duricrust is also present.

LANDFORM FORMATION: The granite, about 1200 million years old, formed when a melted portion of the crust intruded into the surrounding gneiss during continental collision. It slowly cooled under intense pressure, many kilometres below the surface. Over

The granite peaks of the Porongurup Range have a rounded profile

the following millions of years, the landscape was uplifted and eroded, leaving the granite of the Porongurup Range protruding above the surrounding plain. This type of landform, called a monadnock, is isolated because the massive texture of granite is slower to weather and erode than the banded texture of the surrounding gneiss.

NOTABLE FEATURES: Features such as the Devil's Slide mark faults through the granite. Balancing Rock is an example of a granite 'tor'. These form when joints in the granite form blocks that separate from the main rock mass. Over time, the block's corners become rounded by weathering. Sometimes erosion of the supporting material can cause these tors to roll down the side of the range, finishing up well down in the foothills. The flat face of the huge boulder at Castle Rock is caused by the rock breaking along a joint surface. 'The Tree in the Rock' has made use of such a joint, enabling it to get its roots down into the soil and grow on the rock.

The Fitzgerald River National Park is famous for its white spongelite cliffs that are exposed along the Fitzgerald and Hamersley Rivers. These rocks were deposited when a warm sea invaded the landscape some 40 million years ago.

DESCRIPTION: Heath-covered escarpments and flat-topped hills that rise up to 200 metres above sea level are cut by rivers, forming white cliffs commonly banded with brown or red beds.

ROCK TYPES: The rocks, known as the Pallinup Siltstone, are made from the silica skeletons of sponges. This lightweight porous rock is called spongelite and has been used as a valuable building stone at Ravensthorpe and Hopetoun. It is presently being mined at Woogenellup, north-east of Mount Barker, and used as a fire resistant material, pet litter and building stone.

LANDFORM FORMATION: Around 40 million years ago, during the Eocene, the sea level was about 300 metres higher than its present level. The coast was up to 65 kilometres inland, forming a huge embayment that extended from near Albany to Israelite Bay and up to Norseman. Many islands were left within this new warm shallow sea, including the Barrens Ranges, Porongurup Range, and Mount Manypeaks. Sediments rich with the skeletons of sponges slowly settled onto the new seabed, forming a blanket over the area. As the sea level fell again, the rivers draining the hinterland cut deeply into the soft spongelite, forming colourful gorges.

NOTABLE FEATURES: As well as sponges, other forms of marine life such as bivalves, gastropods, echinoids, bryozoans, plant leaves and nautiloids were also preserved as fossils in the spongelite.

Photo – Bill Belson/Lochman Transparencies

Above: *Spongelite, Fitzgerald River*   Below: *Spongelite, Twertup*

Photo – Dennis Sarson/Lochman Transparencies

Along the coast of the Fitzgerald River National Park lies a series of rugged quartzite and schist ranges collectively known as the Barren Ranges. The rocks record layers of sand and silt originally deposited on the sea floor about 1830 million years ago. About 700 million years later, these rocks were caught up in the collision between the Western Australian Craton and the Mawson Craton. They were buried to about 30 kilometres, heated to more than 600°C, and metamorphosed into the rocks we see today. They formed part of the same ancient mountain range that included the Porongurup Range and the granites and gneisses along the south coast (see pages 56-57 and 48-51).

DESCRIPTION: The Barren Ranges are a chain of coastal hills nearly 500 metres above sea level, incised by river valleys covered with rubble and heath. Precipitous cliffs fall steeply into rocky bays and form striking headlands. The hills are a very distinctive landform and are home to many plants found nowhere else in the world. White cliffs of spongelite can be seen between West Mount Barren and Mid Mount Barren (see pages 58-59).

ROCK TYPES: The Ranges are mostly composed of schist, which is a very fissile rock, meaning that it can be broken into thin sheets. This is because it contains lots of mica. Other common minerals include quartz and chlorite, and at East Mount Barren and along West Beach it also contains abundant kyanite, staurolite and garnet. The schist formed when clay minerals in fine-grained rocks such as siltstone and shale were metamorphosed to form mica. The prominent peaks of The Barrens as well as the scarp on its northern boundary, are composed of quartzite. It contains mostly quartz and some mica and chlorite, and at East Mount Barren it also has kyanite and staurolite. Cross bedding and ripples are common, formed from currents when the sandstone, which was transformed into quartzite, was laid down in water.

Above: *Quartzite and schist along the coast* Below: *East Mount Barren*

LANDFORM FORMATION: The Barren Ranges have formed a distinct landform along the southern coastline. This is because the rock types, and patterns of faults and fractures within these ranges, have made them weather quite differently to the surrounding granites and gneisses that formed during the same continental collision (see page 2). For example, the quartzite that forms the peaks contains mostly crystalline quartz, making it a very hard and solid rock that takes a long time to weather. Also, the schist helps to give the Barrens Ranges their distinctive appearance because it is fissile and tends to form quite jagged rocks. Since being exposed at the surface by uplift and erosion of overlying rocks, the Ranges have also been eroded by the action of pounding waves. In the Pleistocene, for example, when the sea level rapidly changed because of the contraction and expansion of the polar icecaps, the sea level was at one time about 80 metres higher than it is today. Waves cut a platform into the slopes, which can still be seen today on East Mount Barren.

NOTABLE FEATURES: Very elongated pebbles within the rocks at East Mount Barren were formed when the rocks were stretched under enormous pressure during the continental collision. This collision also made the rocks bend, forming very angular folds that can commonly be seen in the schist. These are called chevron folds.

Right: *Quartzite and schist along the coast*

Photo – Greg Harold

Wave Rock, near the Wheatbelt town of Hyden, is one of Western Australia's most well known landforms. It rises about 12 metres above the ground, like a giant wave about to break.

DESCRIPTION: The 'wave' is not a separate rock, but an overhanging natural wall more than 100 metres long on the northern side of a large outcrop known as Hyden Rock.

ROCK TYPES: Granite is the main rock type and is around 2600 million years old. It contains quartz, feldspar and mica. The granite is porphyritic, meaning that it contains larger feldspar crystals, or phenocrysts, surrounded by finer grained minerals. There are also faint bands within the rock, known as flow banding. This formed when the magma intruded into the surrounding rocks and started to cool before it stopped moving. Consequently, the minerals that began to crystallise preserved the way the magma flowed.

LANDFORM FORMATION: This type of landform, known as a 'flared slope', is quite a young geological feature that commonly forms in many granite outcrops. The most likely cause of the wave shape is weathering of the rock by groundwater when most of it was covered with sand and soil. Rainwater, running off the outcrop, ponded around its base and very slowly dissolved the underlying rock to form soil. When eventually the soil was stripped away, a smooth concave slope was left, with an adjoining flat pavement.

NOTABLE FEATURES: Along its full length are rusty red, ochre, and sandy grey vertical streaks. These are caused by algal growth. The dark stains are living algae attached to the granite. They change to brown when the water supply disappears and the algae die. Algae that have been dead for a few seasons fall away from the rock, leaving fresh bare granite. Running obliquely from its base to the top of the wave is a wide, straight-sided vein of quartz and

feldspar crystals that is much coarser than the surrounding granite. This is a pegmatite vein that formed from the same magma as the granite, but which contained a large amount of water and intruded soon after the granite had crystallised. The high water content resulted in relatively slow cooling and the growth of large crystals.

Several estuaries, inlets and lakes such as Broke Inlet, Nornalup Inlet, Wilson Inlet, Fitzgerald Inlet and Jerdacuttup Lakes lie along WA's southern coastline. Most of these were old river valleys that were drowned by rising sea levels after the last ice age. Stokes Inlet, in Stokes National Park near Esperance, is a typical example.

DESCRIPTION: Stokes Inlet, covering around 14 square kilometres, is the largest estuary around Esperance and the only one with reasonably deep water. The Young and Lort Rivers flow into the upper reaches of the inlet, but when the water level is low in summer they are cut off from the lagoon by a wide river delta. The estuary mouth lies in the middle of Dunster Castle Bay, also cut off from the sea by a high sand bar. This only breaks every few years, and then only for a few weeks. Long dunes on either side of the estuary parallel the coast.

ROCK TYPES: Seashells, minute marine organisms and quartz make up the high coastal dunes of limestone, shelly sandstone and sand. This coastal strip of very young material is present around much of the South-West as cliffs and rocky headlands (see pages 20-21). Near the mouth of the Young River, within Stokes National Park, are outcrops of gneiss, formed about 1700 million years ago. These distinctive banded rocks were originally igneous rocks, such as granite, granodiorite and pegmatite. When the Western Australian Craton collided with the Mawson Craton between 1345 and 1140 million years ago, these igneous rocks were metamorphosed into gneiss, as a mountain range formed.

LANDFORM FORMATION: Stokes Inlet probably originated as a fault in the gneissic rocks, which was later weathered and eroded by rivers into a deeply incised valley. During the last ice age, when the sea level was more than 100 metres lower than it is today, the inlet was a wide river valley that drained water to the ocean many kilometres to the south. As the icecaps contracted and the sea

Photo – Gordon Roberts

level rose over the last 18 000 years, the river valley was flooded, forming an estuary. The nearby swamps and Lake Cobinup would have been part of this estuary, which was then a marine embayment similar to Princess Royal Harbour near Albany.

During the last few thousand years, waves have moved sand onshore, offshore and alongshore, narrowing the estuary mouth and forming a sand bar at Dunster Castle Bay. Fossil shells indicate that the bar probably started forming about 4 000 years ago. River sediment has collected in the estuary and formed the wide river deltas, the swamps and Lake Cobinup, and shallowed its upper part. The lower part of the estuary is still relatively deep. As a result, the salinity and water level of the inlet varies greatly with river flow and evaporation.

NOTABLE FEATURES: The estuary's mouth is now only 200 metres wide; it has narrowed from the east by a tongue of dune that has probably only recently been stabilised by vegetation, and from the west by a dune that is still mobile. Two lines of nearshore reefs parallel to the ocean beach suggest that the beach and bar were once located further out to sea.

PEAK CHARLES

Towering above the surrounding plain, 130 kilometres north-east of Esperance, is Peak Charles, visible for more than 50 kilometres in all directions.

DESCRIPTION: Essentially a very large and isolated steep-sided dome, or monadnock, rising more than 651 metres above sea level, its weathered surface has dramatic orange and brown hues. To the south is its sister peak, Peak Eleanora. Both peaks lie within the Peak Charles National Park.

ROCK TYPES: Known as the Fitzgerald Peaks Syenite, it contains mostly syenite and granite. The minerals include feldspar, pyroxene, amphibole, biotite mica and quartz. Syenite looks very similar to granite, but has a greater proportion of feldspar and not as much quartz. Together, the peaks form a crescent-shaped mass of rock that crystallised from a single large body of magma, or pluton, which intruded the surrounding granite country rock about 2350 million years ago.

LANDFORM FORMATION: The large size and domed shape of Peak Charles is probably due to the rock having very few open joints compared to those in the surrounding granite into which it intruded. The peak is more resistant to weathering because water cannot easily pass through it and break down the minerals. The surrounding rock, however, had many more fractures that allowed water to penetrate it and weather it away faster than Peak Charles. In places where rocks of the peak are well jointed, they erode into boulders with a rounded shape, known as tors. There are also several well developed 'wave rock' features, accentuated by streaks of black algae. These formed when the rock was partly covered by sand and soil, and groundwater weathered the fresh granite underneath (see pages 64-65).

NOTABLE FEATURES: The rocks contain small rounded darker fragments (mafic rocks) that form ghost-like patches, blebs, lenses and pods, known as xenoliths. These broke off from the

Above: *Syenite at the top of Peak Charles*   Below: *Peak Charles*

Photos – Chris Garnett

country rock deep in the Earth's crust, when the magma intruded into it, and were then preserved within the molten rock. On the slopes of Peak Charles, several wave-cut platforms record an ancient shoreline where sea waves pounded the rocky slopes. This happened about 40 million years ago when Peak Charles was an island in a sea rich with sponges (see page 58).

The Geological Survey of Western Australia (GSWA) is a division of the Western Australian Department of Mineral and Petroleum Resources. For more than 100 years, the GSWA has carried out geoscientific studies of the State, with the aim of revealing its mineral and petroleum wealth. The geoscientific information gathered forms maps, reports, evaluations and data summaries. These help the mineral and petroleum industries, the public and other government departments to carry out exploration, mining and land use planning.

Between 1847 and 1888, a series of Government Geologists were appointed to investigate mineral discoveries in the new Colony. Some of this early work led to the first Western Australian gold rush at Halls Creek in 1885-86. Based on this contribution to the Colony's development, the government eventually recognised the importance of setting up a geological survey. In 1888, headed by Government Geologist Harry Page Woodward, the GSWA was subsequently born, essentially a 'one-man band' with limited funds. Over the next 60 years, although only a handful of staff were added, more than half of Western Australia was mapped, many mining centres investigated and areas of potential mineralisation identified. In 1961, under the direction of Joe Lord, the first systematic mapping of the State began, taking 20 years to complete. This resulted in the first real understanding of the geological framework of Western Australia and set the groundwork for major mineral and petroleum discoveries. During the last 20 years, more detailed studies and mapping have been carried out, resulting in further discoveries and a better understanding of those areas that are most prospective.

The GSWA is now one of the largest and most respected geological surveys in the southern hemisphere, employing nearly 150 staff, including more than 65 geologists, and serves a minerals

Photo – Courtesy of the Geological Survey of WA

and petroleum industry that contributes more than 1000 million dollars a year in royalties.

Geological maps and other publications on the geology of the South-West can be obtained by contacting the Information Centre; Department of Minerals and Petroleum Resources, 100 Plain Street, East Perth, WA 6004, phone (08) 9222 3459, fax (08) 9222 3444, or visit the website (www.mpr.wa.gov.au).

INDEX

The Monadnocks

ABOUT THE AUTHOR

Iain Copp is a geologist and freelance writer/photographer. He worked for many years with the Geological Survey of Western Australia and also in exploration for mineral and petroleum companies.

OTHER BOOKS IN THIS SERIES

Orchids of the South-West
Wildflowers of Shark Bay
Wildflowers of the South Coast
Common Wildflowers of the South-West Forests
Common Wildflowers of the Mid-West
Common Trees of the South-West Forests
Common Trees of the Goldfields
Common Plants of the Kimberley
Common Plants of the Pilbara
Bush Tucker Plants of the South-West
Common Birds in the Backyard
Common Birds of the South-West Forests
Common Birds of the Kimberley
Australian Birds of Prey
Threatened and Rare Birds of Western Australia
Whales and Dolphins of Western Australia
Mammals of the South-West
Mammals of North-Western Australia
Hazardous Animals of North-Western Australia
Animals of Shark Bay
Bugs in the Backyard
Landforms of the Kimberley
Beachcombers Guide to South-West Beaches

ISBN 0-7307-5516-9

9 780730 755166

DEPARTMENT OF
Conservation
AND LAND MANAGEMENT
Conserving the nature of WA

$6.50

COMMON BIRDS

of the South-West Forests

BUSH BOOKS

What bird is that?

Bush Books are a series of practical field guides to help you learn about and discover WA's unique plants, animals and special features, region by region.

ABOUT THE AUTHORS

Carolyn Thomson-Dans is a special projects officer for the Department of Conservation and Land Management. She has written and edited numerous publications about WA's natural environment and wildlife, including *LANDSCOPE* magazine, *Leaf and Branch*, *North-West Bound*, *Mountains of Mystery*, and *Dive and Snorkel Sites in Western Australia*.

John Hunter is a public affairs officer with the Department of Conservation and Land Management and regularly writes the *Urban Antics* section in *LANDSCOPE* magazine. John has had a long time interest and involvement in natural history and, as a result, has a very wide-ranging knowledge of the State's wildlife.

Publisher: Department of Conservation and Land Management, 17 Dick Perry Avenue, Kensington, Western Australia, 6151.
Managing Editor: Ron Kawalilak.
Editor: Carolyn Thomson-Dans.
Technical Advisers: Kevin Coate, Grant Wardell-Johnson, Ron Johnstone, Mike Craig, John Dell.
Design and production: Sandra van Brugge, Maria Duthie.
Photography: Babs and Bert Wells/Department of Conservation and Land Management, unless otherwise indicated.
Front cover: Red-tailed black-cockatoo. Photo by Robert Garvey.

ISBN 0 73096997 5
First published in 1996
Reprinted in 2002
© CALM 2002